What to do with this life?

Cole Van Atter- Burns

Presentation by *BookLeaf Publishing*

Web: www.bookleafpub.com

E-mail: info@bookleafpub.com

ISBN: 9789357690935

First edition 2022

PREFACE

My aim is to help people who have struggled whether that be with a mental illness or the questioning of their sexuality. To put into perspective that you aren't alone in your struggles.

Mid-September

Hazy is the mind on a rainy day
Thoughts spread through the pages of my brain.
I still can't seem to keep them still.
Words said
I continue to feel like they aren't being heard.
Stuck behind this door
Pushing, pounding, and clawing.
My voice only reaches the other side in the form
of a whisper.

It Wouldn't Be Like This If I Were A Man

Holding my girlfriend's hand in public let's
people know we're together.
You would think
Until random strangers come up and tell her
their friend likes her.

Up My Sleeve

Maybe I have something up my sleeve.
Other than predictable feelings
Always pleasing
Making time for myself
Then what's left for everyone else?
All of my reasons tugging on each other until I
burst.
Flowing streams of melancholy
I wipe them away.
Today I have a couple tricks up my sleeve.
I crack a joke
All smiles until the clouds roll back in.
With a bit of thunder and lighting of course .
Would you expect anything less from a woman
with multiple complexities?
Written by walking degrees in white jackets.

You Could Tell

You can feel everything all at once.
You're just that person
The one who picks me up when I'm slowly
falling.
Trying to stitch things back together.
"You didn't make that tear" you state.
It doesn't seem like anyone else is going to
mend it.
"It's not all on you to defend it".
Looking down
I set it aside
You could tell?
I thought I was the only one.

Blue

5

The light shines through the blue suede curtain.
Lifeless I lay wondering how I can make the
days go faster.
I get into a funk where I don't know what to do
with myself.
My brain moves a mile a minute
All I can do is lay
I try and focus on the light shining through,
rather than the darkness that consumes.

Friends

Sorrow flows through me
I don't have many friends to console me.
I'm not very social
the friends I have had, weren't who I thought
they were.
Loneliness has swindled me.
I wonder if the people who have loads of friends
feel this way.
Are they lonely too?
Perhaps they are
Surrounded by so many people
That they feel as though loneliness has swindled
them too.

Things I Don't Like

7

I don't like thinking about certain demons from
your past.
Every time I do I want it to be the last.
No matter how hard I wish it wasn't a timeline
you've endured.
It was
Fair didn't even ask you.
I would take those years away from you.
I know no matter how hard I wish, it still won't
come true.

Mind Race

My mind speaks such horrible things to me
I wouldn't speak to anyone that way.
So cruel and so weak
I didn't notice I was gritting my teeth
Squinting my eyes
Touching my tongue to the roof of my mouth
Palms sweating
My thoughts never stop
always so loud
Silence on the outside
Chaos inside

Run

9

Perhaps running that extra mile was the hardest
thing you've had to do.
I'm glad you did.

Anniversary Number 2

I love you with all of my heart.
It's hard to spend even one night apart.
With you my soul is complete.
Matched perfectly
Will you have me for as long as you want me?
Is eternity and after too long to ask for?
Without you I would melt into my surroundings.
Torn apart from a broken heart.
Say you will have me.
I promise you all I have to give and more
If you like.

Communication

Conflict
Something that can be so pointless at times.
Only solved by communication.
Effective
It's key
To new beginnings
Long awaited ends
As simple as a misunderstanding
Imagine what you could do with effective
communication.
Still, some choose not to
Do you?

I Know You Try To Not Be

Sometimes your so judging of yourself it makes
my heart ache.
A sad pace
You are magnificent
Your stomach
Your arms and legs
Thighs and hips
Entangle to shape you
Your body
It holds your spirit
Which is an honor
And it knows that
I know that
You should too
You're gorgeous in every single way.
Everyone knows that
I look at you and I know that you try too.
I wish that you could look through my eyes.
Maybe then you would see
You are the most beautiful person there is.

That Feeling Again

Here comes that feeling again
The one that says I don't belong.
Claims of being friendless
Unimportant
A plain hot mess.
Too thick
Too curvy
Too heavy
All made to make me feel like I should crumble.
Instead, I think I'll stand my ground.
Call myself pretty and worthy.
Until it passes by once more.

Down The Hatch

These pills I have to take everyday
To feel like you
You who can walk into a crowded room
Without a single thought of who's around you.
No protruding thoughts of worst-case scenarios.
No shaky hands or sweaty palms.
Oh, you don't rehearse the words that will come
out of your mouth next.
How fast is the beating of your chest?
The panic that comes out of nowhere that warns
you to leave.
Or else
Hmm, maybe that just me.
I fear that I will have to take these pills
indefinitely.

The Thing About Being A Woman

The thing about being a woman
People will think you're a man hater for pointing
out inequality.
When really you're just sick of the injustice.
Men get paid more than Woman.
In 2022
It's true
The conversation has been on pause
Same as women's rights for access to
contraception.
Why aren't men's rights to contraception being
questioned?
Or why they get paid so much more than a
woman in the same position?
But nobody wants to talk about that.
When a man gets a promotion it's well deserved
When a women gets a promotion they should be
getting paid more.

Breeze of Thought

Sunrise
Or
Sunset
Emotions never rest
Swift like the wind
They take me through the trees
Leaves
Falling to the bed of the earth
My heart hurts because I never rest.
Sunrise or sunset
The breeze is always blowing
My mind endlessly flowing
One tree to the next

People Pleaser

To please everyone is impossible
Still I try
I should work more on myself
But what about when you need help?
I'll be right there with the gift of me
Should you need it
All it will cost you is nothing
Except for me
It will cost me
Later on, I fear
I may not be able to stop helping
I would tear out my eyes
Just in case you needed them to see.
You don't have to give them back
As long as you are alright
Well then
I am too

Before Speaking

Before you speak
Think about how it may affect the recipient
Will it be perceived how you mean?
Or will it sting?
Be left on the brain
Linger longer than you please.

What Lies Beneath

Between the lines of my mind
Lie my thoughts of which no one can see.
Although some can hear
Even when I do not speak.

My Shadow

At times my shadow doesn't move with me.
I grab it
Trying to put it back into sync.
It wants to move faster than my progress will
allow.
I know it wants to start a life with objects I can't
buy.
I'm not there yet
I reach into my pockets, pull them out and find
not a single dime.

Life Changes

Life is always changing
The seasons
Feelings
Family
People will come
They will go
Change
Ones you've known for years.
Your mind will evolve
The times
You
Will change
It's up to you if it's for the better.

www.ingramcontent.com/pod-product-compliance
Lightning Source LLC
Chambersburg PA
CBHW070736160726
48003CB00006BA/2541